Liquid Sky

Jennifer Gurney

ISBN: 978-93-6354-121-4

First Edition: 2025
Rs. 200/-

Cyberwit.net
HIG 45 Kaushambi Kunj, Kalindipuram
Allahabad - 211011 (U.P.) India
http://www.cyberwit.net
Tel: +(91) 9415091004
E-mail: info@cyberwit.net

Printed at Repro India Limited.

Contents

Previously published in The Ravens Perch on 8-9-23

We Are Never Ready

We are never ready
For the call
No matter how often
We tell ourselves we are.

It comes
Unbidden
In the night
To hijack our hearts
And render us
Bereft

In the movie theater
Of our life
Reliving
Rewatching
Memories of the one we lost.

As if their life is the Sunday matinee
That we just bought
A ticket to

And side movies begin to play
Concurrently
Of all the lives they
Touched and intertwined with

All the blessings they bestowed
Upon all of us they touched

And the sense of loss is
Deafening
Like a white noise
I've only heard before
When death has taken
others whom I
I cherish

And here again
I step into
the shoes of grief
Not purchased
Not desired
Yet they fit
And they are mine
And somehow I know them

They are my shoes to wear
Until this loss
Can be absorbed.
They will carry me through
Until the fresh waves
Of loss
Wash over me
And the salt water of grief
Holds me
In its swells and surges
Rising and falling
In its own pattern
Not of my making

But for me to feel
To process
To withstand

Until my feet can rest on solid ground
Once again

For grief will find me
All the days
Of the rest of my life.
Of that I am certain.
It is truly the price
We pay for the
Honor of loving.

I now know that this grief, too,
Will patina with age
As time and prayer
And memory and love
Stitch my sore, tender heart
Back together anew
With the stitches becoming scars
Where my heart has been
Torn open with grief

I know I will mend.

And

Alongside the grief -
Buried in the grief
Somehow -
Each day onward

There will be endless gratitude for
All that she was
All that she imparted
All that she gave
And the honor
That I got to be
Her granddaughter
Her goddaughter
Her friend
For 58 years
On this planet
And, still, in a way
In my core
For the rest of my life

And moving through grief
Honoring her life
By how I seek to live mine
will be my life journey
From this day forth.

For that is
how much
I loved her.

For that is
How much
I love her still.

Previously published in The Ravens Perch on 6-27-23

Observations of Pelicans on the Lake One Day

Pelicans.

Elusive
There one minute
Gone the next
Just gone

Behind the reeds
Flash of white
Then hidden again

Emerging again
To be seen,
Admired,
Studied.

Fishing
Tipping over
Silent
Yet active
Eating
Are they cooperating
In their fishing?
Like dolphins who circle
to stir up the fish?

Do they sense that
I'm trying to watch them?

Awkward bodies
Yet graceful
As they dive

Funny yellow-orange beaks
Must be distinctive
Ardent with their
Poking into the water

Shoulder to shoulder
They hunt
9-foot wingspan
All tucked up
Together
Underneath
As they float
And glide

And they're gone
Enigmatic
Elusive

Pelicans.

Previously published in Cattails in October 2024

Backseat

Mama, why is the sky blue? When will we be home? Can we have spaghetti-os for dinner? Where do tears come from? Did you bring any more snacks? Can we go to the park after dinner and have popsicles and ride our bikes and stay out till the lights come on like last time? How does a wind turbine work? Can we read two chapters of Harry Potter tonight instead of one? What's an allowance? Where do you go when you die? Why do people have to die anyways? Why can't people and dogs and stuffed animals live forever? Mama, why is the sky blue?

one by one
his questions unpacked
the universe

Previously published in Lothlorien on 10-27-24

I Noticed

I noticed
the silkiness of your fur
beneath my fingers

I noticed
when I could let sadness go
love flooded in

I noticed
that your life with me
played like a movie

as you snuggled
deep into the cover
on my lap

I noticed
the deep kindness of the vet
who came to help

a gentleness of spirit
walked in the door
with him

coaching us through
with knowledge and
infinite grace

I noticed
that I spoke to you
in poetry

thanking you
for 17 years of
love and friendship

giving you permission
to step into the
gloaming

and run free
in the garden
forever

I noticed
how my friend showed love
by being present

calmly supporting
us both through this difficult
yet magical moment

kissing you goodbye
holding my hand
hearing our stories

I noticed
how deeply you relaxed
into your final breaths

I noticed
a gentle peace settling in
as you transitioned

I noticed
my hand still petting you
even after you'd gone

knowing I should stop
but not yet being
able to

I noticed
your collar was still warm
as I held it, after

I noticed
how quiet the house seemed
then

I noticed
how the tears flowed
of their own accord

I noticed
your hairs in the dryer
lint catcher, today

I noticed
how my other cat and I
are finding our new normal

I noticed
that I still see you
in my periphery

I noticed
that coming home
I still call your name

I noticed
that I still listen
for your footfall

and I cat still feel
your silky fur
beneath my fingers

I noticed
that you filled a very large space
for such a tiny cat

Previously published by Lothlorien on 10-27-24

The Holy Spirit Knocked on My Door

the Holy Spirit
knocked on my door
twice yesterday
once in a friend
once in a vet

they filled my home
with pure, calm love
allowing me
such grace and
understanding

coaching me
to be pure love for one
who's been pure love for me
until she breathed
her last

after

one wrapped you
in a blanket with such
compassion
that it lifted
my soul

the other wrapped me
in love
and stayed for dinner
and overnight
so I wouldn't be alone

I'm grateful
for the Holy Spirit
knocking on my door
and for having the courage
to open it

Previously published in The Ravens Perch on 10-28-24

Melting Pot

I was blessed to grow up in a multicultural neighborhood in Kalamazoo, Michigan in the 60s and 70s. Our one block had families from India, China, Turkey, the Netherlands and three African American families. Neighborhood potlucks were an adventure. Daily life was varied and interesting. Like the time our neighbor taught belly dancing to all the neighbors' kids on the front lawn. I didn't realize at the time how unusual this was for the place and time. I'm grateful.

all the cultures
mixing together
block party

Previously published in The Ravens Perch on 10-28-24

To Forgive, Divine

Poverty robs the innocent of a meal, a bed, a job. How does one forgive poverty?

on my food bank shift
you turn down a can of beans
so another can have it

Terminal illness robs countless people of a future. How does one forgive illness and death?

your pictures
with a scarf instead of hair
get me every time

War rips our world apart and forces us to choose sides. How does one forgive war?

Picasso's dove
tattooed on my heart
will this give peace a chance?

Previously published in The Ravens Perch on 12-8-24

Friday the 13th

The patio door was open a crack, so my cat could chase bugs outside. I sat on the couch for just a moment, but somehow fell asleep for a bit. I'll blame it on the COVID vaccine I'd just gotten. I awoke to a rustling, and discovered a big black cat in my house. I shooed it outside and looked for my cat, whom I thought had been scared away. I looked for hours, all around the house, around the patio, throughout the neighborhood. I shook his food box and called for him. Just when it was growing dark, and I'd begun to give up hope, he sauntered down the stairs for supper. He'd been hiding from the other cat this whole time.

superstitions
can make you think
all sorts of crazy things

Previously published in The Ravens Perch on 12-8-24

Left Behind

When you left, you took a piece of me with you – the center of my heart. The place where trust dwells. The hollow where hope blooms. The nook where dreams are born. You might not even know that you packed it with your record albums, Harley Davidson and power tools. When you unpack your last box and discover it, can you mail it back to me, please?

nestled in a box
wrapped in bubble wrap
my heart

Previously published in The Ravens Perch on 12-8-24

Wide Open Spaces

Who am I when I am all that remains? My mother has gone … and I am motherless. My grandmother, too. Is grandmotherless even a word? My soul-cat has gone before me … and I am hollow. My soulmate, lover, best friend, husband, has left … and I am bereft. Who am I when I am all that remains?

newly blooming
layers on layers, opening
my true self

Previously published in The Ravens Perch on 12-9-24

In the Wee Small Hours

The cool, dark air met me as I opened the garage door and wheeled out the bins. My slippers flapping on the concrete, I glanced up at my neighbor's house and saw an unexpected sight. Serendipity.

sliver moon
reflected perfectly
in your window

Previously published in The Ravens Perch 12-10-24

I Hope It's You

I think I might have finally
Lived long enough of life
The losses and the pleasures
The pain and the joy
The disappointments and regrets
To finally have something
Valuable to say.

Or if not valuable,
Maybe just … needed.
Is it me who needs to say it
Or you who needs to hear it?
It doesn't really matter which.

If nothing more than
Please know that
Your pain
Is survivable.
There is an end to it.
Although it may feel
Like it will consume you
And break you,
Smother you with its
Ferocity,
Break you,
There is another side
To this dark tunnel.

You can do this.
You can survive this.
You can live again.

On the other side
After you have
Endured and healed
You can
Grow and even blossom.
Because you took the time
To listen to your heart.
Found the people whom you trust
To confide in.
Did the work that you
Fought for longer than
An eternity
But finally gave in

Because to not do the work
Left you mired in the pain.
And ultimately
discovered the things that
Fill you up.

So you are whole again
In a new way
With your heart stitched together
But stronger,
Somehow.
You are newly-brave
Tentatively stepping into
Your new self.
Tiptoeing into your

New life with your
Just-now-mended heart.
But you're doing it.
And it's remarkable.

Keep doing it.
And do it again
The next time
Life goes sideways.

And again.
And again.

Only these times
Don't fight the work of healing
For so long.
Because we all face
This challenge.
These challenges.
Sometimes big ones
All at once.
Or back-to-back.
It is part and parcel
Of being human.

To feel
Means we'll get hurt.
To love
Means we'll grieve.
To love deeply
Means the grief we feel
Will be almost
Unbearable.

But not completely.
Because we are still here.

No one tells us this.
They feed us the fairytale.

But I will tell you the truth.
Life is hard.
There is exhausting work to do
To get through it.
It will happen again
And again.
When we feel we can least
Handle it.
It's not our choice.
We don't get to decide
When our lives turn upside down.

But
Despite it all
I know in the very center of my core:
You can do it.
It's worth it.
You are worth it.

Maybe even if just one
Person needs to hear this
It will all be worth it.

I hope it's you.

Previously published in The Ravens Perch on 12-10-24

Morning Walk

scattered heart rocks
magenta sweet pea bursting
memories of you

an owl overhead
the river's song
memories of you

sunshine
bark's depth
memories of you

peacefulness
walking beside my tree friends
memories of you

cotton on the path
sticking to remnants of rain
memories of you

mourning dove's call
milkweed ready to burst
memories of you

shadows of cool
clouds floating, drifting
memories of you

a swing on a tree
dandelion wishes waiting
memories of you

a moth on a buttercup
tall grass waving in the breeze
memories of you

the path's curve
where I last heard your voice
memories of you

Previously published in The Ravens Perch on 12-10-24

Thinking

I love learning how the brain works.
I think it's cool that when we learn
about how the brain works,
we're actually using the brain
to learn about the brain.

Did you know that memories
are not stored intact, in one place?
They're dismantled and stored
in the various sensory locations.
Then, when one of those
aspects is triggered,
the various other sensory memories
are teased and the memory emerges
wholly formed.
That's why when we hear a song on the radio,
it can trigger strong memories.
Or why when I wake to the smell of coffee,
I'm instantly transported to my grandma's house.

The implications are great.
It's the very basis of multisensory,
hands-on learning,
which is at the core of my
constructivist educational philosophy.
So much of traditional education is based
on the lecture/note taking format.

Students "sit and get" or do a worksheet.
But they don't learn this way.
They have to interact with the material
in order to construct their meaning.
And when they use multiple senses,
the brain stores the memories in more locations,
making it easier to retrieve the information
when needed.

Costa and Kollick's Habits of Mind
also teach us about the brain.
These are the 16 learning dispositions
that make for successful people of all ages.
One of my favorites is metacognition.
When we think deeply about our thinking,
we are much more reflective.
We have to question, ponder, ruminate,
connect, infer, wonder.
Metacognition moves us higher
on the Bloom's taxonomy of higher-level thinking,
from merely remembering to understanding,
applying, analyzing, evaluating and even creating.
It is in thinking about our thinking
that the growth lies.

We even have the power to
change our thinking and
even to change our brains.
Instead of letting our thinking run
full course when we face uncomfortable situations,
the book Efficacy Therapy challenges us to
stop, relax and regroup.
It's a healthy reminder that we can,

in fact, change the way our brains work.
Our brain is an organ,
is alive and
we have the power to train it in
whatever direction we want.

Why not go somewhere positive?
Like something as substantial as
learning a musical instrument,
or something a bit lighter,
like maybe a new card game?
Then, we can
ponder, reflect, wonder and …
tackle the big stuff, like
effective problem solving.
Prodigious.

Previously published in Ravens Perch on 12-10-24

No Words

I have
no words
and a million
to describe
this
shimmering moment
my mind seeks
for a means to describe
yet it's my heart who steals the pen
for to capture
a moment of true perfection
requires the eyes of the soul
as bliss alights
for a millisecond
on this orbiting world of life
and then
quick as it came
it's gone
but not really
for good life is lived
in the reflection of these moments
I have
no words
and a million
to describe
this
shimmering moment

Previously published in Retrograde Review on 12-12-24

Safekeeper

When all who have known me have gone, who will keep the memories of me alive? Will my children's children's children have heard stories about me, although they will never have met me? Will I be kept alive through their storytelling? Will I live on through my poetry, still read in the years after I'm gone? Will my paintings live on in the homes of those who were born after I died? Or will I be the face in the photograph someone asks one day, "Anyone know who this is?" as everyone present shakes their head. In honor of this phenomenon, I will try to be a better keeper of the memories of those who have gone before me. To pass on the torch of memories to those who come after me. I can become the toggle switch of memory. The fulcrum point of time.

stirring the ashes
the embers of memory ignite
sparking a fire

Previously published in Folk Ku Issue 4, 2025.

now
you are only a poem
in my notebook

Previously published in Folk Ku Issue 4, 2025.

running in and out
of the ocean
wave boy

Previously published in The Daily Verse in January 2025.

the number of
planes buzzing overhead
now outnumbers
the clouds, the birds
even the stars

Previously published in Cold Moon Journal November 2024

days shortening
little by little
leaning into fall

Previously published in Fresh Out October 2024

leaves
crunch under foot . . . .
foot fall

Previously published in Fresh Out October 2024

fall, bittersweet
new episodes for all the shows
I binge-watch

Previously published in Five Fleas on 10-24-24

if only
I could lose loss
and find found

Previously published in LEAF Magazine Issue 5, December 2024

the gray crayon
still with its pointy end
only blue skies

Previously published in LEAF Magazine Issue 5, December 2024

first golden leaf
on a summer-morning walk
autumn budges in

Previously published in Five Fleas on 10-27-24

getting my brave on
I step into
the fray

Previously published in Five Fleas on 10-27-24

I wonder
what happens to all the poems
written only in my mind

Previously published in Lothlorien on 10-27-24

the vet's voice
softly shares the test results
my heart disintegrates

Previously published in Lothlorien on 10-27-24

when it's time
to call the vet again
I pray to be brave

Previously published in Lothlorien on 10-27-24

I empty my heart
of sadness and fear
love floods in

Previously published in Lothlorien on 10-27-24

as you relaxed
warm on my lap
my soul breathed

Previously published in Lothlorien on 10-27-24

in that moment
you stepped into the gloaming
forever

Previously published in Lothlorien on 10-27-24

thanking you
for 17 years of love
as you slipped through
the slats of the garden
and ran free

Previously published in Lothlorien on 10-27-24

a piece of my heart
goes with you into
the gentle, soft night

a piece of your heart
stays with me and rises
with the dawn

Previously published in Lothlorien on 10-27-24

it was an honor
to love and be loved
in return

Previously published in Five Fleas on 10-30-24

just
beneath the surface
the truth

Previously published in Five Fleas on 10-30-24

stepping into
the vast wilderness...
I meet myself

Previously published in Five Fleas on 11-20-24

endless lies
the pattern
of misogyny

Previously published in Gabriel's Horns Books Music Anthology in November 2024

my best cleaning—
to loud rock music and the
pressure of company

Previously published in Gabriel's Horns Books Music Anthology in November 2024

name charm clinking
against her water bowl
music

Previously published in Gabriel's Horns Books Music Anthology in November 2024

I see your breath
in the candle's flame
dancing to night's music

Previously published in Gabriel's Horns Books Music Anthology in November 2024

Mozart fills the air
with musical brilliance from
centuries ago

Previously published in Gabriel's Horns Books Music Anthology in November 2024

front porch
rowdy thunderstorm
summer music

Previously published in Different Truths in December 2024

falling asleep
I catch myself
awake

Previously published in Different Truths in December 2024

nothing makes me feel
more like an artist
paint on my fingers

Previously published in Different Truths in December 2024

the canvas calls to me
never afraid of
all that white

Previously published in Different Truths in December 2024

each meteor
streaking across inky sky
a wish fulfilled

Previously published in Different Truths in December 2024

hanging in the sky
one with the clouds
in flight

Previously published in Different Truths in December 2024

picturing Dad's face
searching the crowd for me
I am loved

Previously published in Different Truths in December 2024

swallowing doubt
she gets her brave on
for the day

Previously published in Different Truths in December 2024

every shadow
light behind it
to be seen

Previously published in Different Truths in December 2024

floating on the day
your hand slips into mine
harvesting the moment

Previously published in Different Truths in December 2024

even when
the river runs dry
you slake me

Previously published in Five Fleas on 11-28-24

the sound
of November-December
whoosh

Previously published in Five Fleas on 11-28-24

nothingness
the universe
bang

Previously published in Shadow Pond Issue IV December 2024

finding its way in
through the tiniest of cracks
love

Previously published in The Daily Verse in January 2025

one after another
poems nascent in my heart
newly born

Previously published in The Daily Verse in January 2025

a poem leaks out
through the threadbare spot
of my newly healing heart

Forthcoming in The Daily Verse in January 2025

between the margins
a word here, there
before a patch seals it closed

Hatching

held you in my hand
as a Brownie troop watched
you hatch to the world

peeping from inside
as you pecked your way outside
bit by tiny bit

we watched in awe
as your shell bits fell away
new life emerging

Stepping Into Summer

stepping into summer
like a comfortable pair of jeans

hiking in early morning coolness
coffee on the porch, with birdsong

painting, when it suits me
watering the garden

escaping through books this year
instead of by plane or road trip

long cooking jags,
creating and playing in the kitchen

binging on shows and movies
letting words flow through poetry and prose

riding in the mountains,
the canyons and rivers balm for my soul

playing the piano with windows wide open
listening to opera on the patio at sunset

tennis against a backboard,
feeling the power of each stroke

being among nature
restoring my peace

yoga on the lawn,
with the stretch and pull of muscles

watching a bird's nest
being built on my porch

puzzle books and lemonade, the ice clinking in the glass
word games my grandma passed down by oral tradition

connecting with family and friends
by phone and virtualness

more time outdoors in the sun
breathing in warmth, soaking up contentment

seeking adventures
in my own backyard

marshmallows over the firepit
camping out overnight

letting each day unfold, unplanned
open ended, diaphanous

stepping into summer
like a comfortable pair of jeans

A Piece of My Soul

a little piece of
my soul is in each painting
right on the canvas

it is surprising
to see it unfold, right there
in technicolor

hard to describe ... but ...
like looking in a mirror
and seeing a friend

it used to feel so
vulnerable, being so
transparent in paint

but now, I marvel
at what comes out when the paint
touches the paper

the joy that exudes
even when I'm so troubled
light amidst darkness

art does truly heal
the painter and the paintee
souls connect through art

Last Words

I just realized
I don't know what your
last words were

I wasn't there
by your side to hear them
as you breathed your last

COVID intervened
on our plans for my trip
for your birthday

you were asleep
for your last few days
morphine eased your path

I hope your words
were good ones, like you
of love and kindness

probably thanking
someone for a small gesture
that was your way

or a prayer
whispered gently
to the darkness

I hope your last words
were soft ones, calm ones
probably "I'm ready"

you've been gone
two years now, Mom
and I miss you so

I wish I could have
held your hand as you breathed
your last

my last words to you
would have been
I love you

The Quilt I Made for You

beneath our clasped hands
lies the quilt I made for your
birthday three years past.

colors of springtime
our shared favorite - purple
flowers, butterflies

to remind you of
happy times in your garden,
outside in the sun.

it rests over you
and holds you close, in between
times when I am there.

Stutter Breaths

they catch me off guard
those stutter breaths, after a
good, long crying jag

they're a staccato
response to intensity
of feelings expressed

as if my lungs are
trying to tell me, slow down
just breathe, my dear, breathe

Midnight Sky

My heart yearns for it
In rapt anticipation
Unabashed joy

Minutes turn to hours
As I wait, eyes peeled to see
Streaks across the sky

Boldly proclaiming
Lightness to the midnight sky
Hope for all who see

Remembering a Dream

woke up
with a dream fresh in my mind
which hardly ever happens
anymore

I had set down
all my possessions
a backpack
sleeping bag
money
photographs
all outside the library
because it wasn't open yet

and gone, inexplicably
to a party
with friends I'd been staying with

in hindsight
I clearly wondered
why not bring
all that stuff with me

but in the dream
it all made perfect sense
library
safe place
I'd come back for it later

so then I went to the party
quite fun
most everyone I know
was there

I asked my host
for a ride to my next
destination
I'm not quite sure where it was
just the feeling that
I needed to be there
and that I needed a ride
because I couldn't carry everything at once
by myself

poor planning on my part
she'd already had several
glasses of wine and declined

I was so hurt in the dream
went around to say goodbye
to everyone else
but her

when I returned to the library
all of my earthly possessions
were gone
I was devastated
searching everywhere

I found other bags rifled through
but not mine
I went in the

open library to inquire
and as I pulled open the door
I woke up

what was I thinking
leaving my stuff outside
but the silver lining
was I could travel easier

I woke with equal parts
sadness for the imagined loss
and relief that
all had been undisturbed

so many layers
and lessons
to unravel
as my day unfolds

Liquid Sky

when I hike to the lake
I feel like liquid sky

nothing separates me
from the sand below
from the ancient beaches
that covered the land
in this state that
is now a desert

nothing separates me
from my sister trees
whose bark I know
better than the voice
in my own heart
whose roots grow deeper
than the generations on
anyone's family tree

or the deer who frolick near
knowing I am friend not foe
and can be trusted
as they nestle in the shade
to gain strength for their
next long journey

or the clouds that hold
the water that will fall
and slake my very thirst

I taste the raindrop
that once fell on an ancient leaf
now fossilized
for millions of years

nothing separates me
from the air that breathes around me
holding echoes of voices past
calling to each other
to their foremothers
to my great-great granddaughters to be

nothing separates us
we are all here
in this moment

I descend to rest
upon the lake's shore
that has always been here
and will be forevermore

I smile a long, contented smile
that feels like a stretch after a
winter-long nap

when I am at the lake
I am liquid sky

longing
to see you
face-to-face

breathe in
breathe out
facing the new year

I was there
when you grew your wings
beginning your ascent

ten minutes until your call
equal parts butterflies and
Christmas morning

time is amorphous–
a lifetime passes
in a moment

leaning into
a steep incline, imagining
the view

in unison, yet
a cacophony of voices
pledge of allegiance

clouds clear
and sun shines forth
grief lessens its stronghold

my footprints
leave an impression in the sand
beach signature

Liquid Sky is dedicated to Todd Gurney, the love of my life.

www.ingramcontent.com/pod-product-compliance
Lightning Source LLC
LaVergne TN
LVHW091117150826
845673LV00002B/864

* 9 7 8 9 3 6 3 5 4 1 2 1 4 *